Published by Creative Education
and Creative Paperbacks
P.O. Box 227, Mankato, Minnesota 56002
Creative Education and Creative Paperbacks
are imprints of The Creative Company
www.thecreativecompany.us

Design by The Design Lab
Production by Joe Kahnke
Art direction by Rita Marshall
Printed in the United States of America

Photographs by Alamy (imageBROKER), Corbis (W.
Perry Conway, Sebastian Kennerknecht/Minden Pictures,
Jim Zuckerman), Creative Commons Wikimedia (Tony
Wills), Dreamstime (Alantunnicliffe, Brett Critchley,
Davemhuntphotography, Miroslav Thiele, Sally Wallis,
Arman Zhenikeyev), iStockphoto (Missing35mm, RON-
SAN4D), SuperStock (Gerard Lacz Images)

Library of Congress Cataloging-in-Publication Data
Riggs, Kate.
5574
Falcons / Kate Riggs.
p. cm. — (Amazing animals)
Summary: A basic exploration of the appearance, be-
havior, and habitat of falcons, Earth's fast-flying birds
of prey. Also included is a story from folklore explain-
ing why peregrine falcons are such good fliers.
Includes bibliographical references and index.
ISBN 978-1-60818-753-9 (hardcover)
ISBN 978-1-62832-361-0 (pbk)
ISBN 978-1-56660-795-7 (eBook)
1. Falcons—Juvenile literature.
QL696.F34 R54 2017
598.9/6—dc23   2016004786

CCSS: RI.1.1, 2, 4, 5, 6, 7; RI.2.2, 5, 6, 7, 10;
RI.3.1, 5, 7, 8; RF.1.1, 3, 4; RF.2.3, 4

First Edition HC 9 8 7 6 5 4 3 2 1
First Edition PBK 9 8 7 6 5 4 3 2 1

FALCONS

BY KATE RIGGS

CREATIVE EDUCATION • CREATIVE PAPERBACKS

Peregrine falcons are found all around the world

The 39 kinds of falcons are **birds of prey**. They live on every **continent** except Antarctica. Some falcons are called kestrels or hobbies.

birds of prey birds that hunt and eat other animals

continent one of Earth's seven big pieces of land

A falcon's beak and claws are like knives

A falcon's beak is curved and sharp. Its feet have **talons**. Like other birds, the falcon has feathers. Its wing feathers are very long. Fast falcons can soar high up in the air.

talons the sharp claws of birds of prey

Female falcons are larger than males. The female gyrfalcon (*JER-fal-kin*) is about two feet (0.6 m) long. But the gyrfalcon's wings can stretch more than five feet (1.5 m) across. The smallest kind of falcon is only seven inches (17.8 cm) long. That is about the size of a pencil!

Gyrfalcons live in high mountains and cold, snowy places

The New Zealand falcon is found on the islands of that country

Falcons live in almost every **habitat** on Earth. They stay away from places that are too wet or too cold. Many falcons live near wooded areas and water sources.

habitat a place where animals live

Birds of prey eat meat. Falcons catch mice, birds, bats, and other small animals. They have to land before they can eat. A falcon does not have teeth. So it uses its beak to shred meals.

Falcons swallow everything from feathers to bones

*Eyases have a fluffy
coat of down at first*

A female and male falcon scrape out a nest together. The female lays three to five eggs. **Eyases** come out of the eggs in about 40 days. Young falcons fight over food. They grow quickly and learn to fly. Before they leave the nest, falcons are called fledglings.

eyases baby falcons

Falcons are the fastest animals on Earth. They use their powerful wings to slice through the air. A peregrine falcon can dive at 200 miles (322 km) per hour!

*Falcons soar above prey
before they get ready to dive*

Adult falcons do not have many threats. Larger hawks sometimes hunt them. Humans do, too. Falcons that stay safe can live up to 15 years in the wild.

American kestrels will nest in boxes people make for them

Some people train falcons. They use the birds to hunt. Falcons will hold on to prey until the hunter picks it up. Look for these strong birds as they dive and fly!

Someone who trains falcons is known as a falconer

A *Falcon* Story

Why is the falcon such a fast flier? American Indians in the southeastern United States thought the peregrine falcon was special. They believed it could fly from the upper world of the gods to Earth. The falcon had to fly fast and be strong. People dressed up like falcons to try to be powerful warriors, like falcons.

gods beings thought to have special powers and control over the world

FALCONS

Read More

Hoena, Blake. *Everything Birds of Prey*. Washington, D.C.: National Geographic, 2015.

Riggs, Kate. *Eagles*. Mankato, Minn.: Creative Education, 2012.

Websites

Idaho Public Television: Birds of Prey
http://idahoptv.org/sciencetrek/topics/birds_of_prey/
Watch a show about birds of prey to learn more.

National Geographic Kids: Peregrine Falcon
http://kids.nationalgeographic.com/animals/peregrine-falcon/#peregrine
-falcon-wings-extended.jpg
Find out how a peregrine falcon compares with humans in terms of its speed and other fun facts.

Note: Every effort has been made to ensure that the websites listed above are suitable for children, that they have educational value, and that they contain no inappropriate material. However, because of the nature of the Internet, it is impossible to guarantee that these sites will remain active indefinitely or that their contents will not be altered.

Index